C. Barsotti's

TEXAS

Foreword by Bill Porterfield

Texas Monthly Press, Inc.
P.O. Box 1569
Austin, Texas 78767

A B C D E F G H

Library of Congress Cataloging-in-Publication Data

Barsotti, C. (Charles)
Barsotti's Texas.

1. Texas—Caricatures and cartoons. 2. American wit and humor, Pictorial. I. Porterfield, Bill.
II. Title. III. Title: Texas.
F387.B37 1986 976.4'00207 85-28825
ISBN 0-87719-035-6

Cover design by David Kampa

For Ramoth, Joan, and Jim.

FOREWORD
by Bill Porterfield

Charley used to doodle a lot. At least, that's what we called it, not realizing the purpose that was there all along. Charley was probably as much in the dark about it as the rest of us. Here we'd be sitting in sociology class, listening to Dr. Grusendorff lecture on the pros and cons of heredity versus environment, and there would be Barsotti, stubby pencil in hand, a lank shock of dark hair obscuring half his face, taking his own peculiar note of what was coming down. It was in the early fifties at Southwest Texas State in San Marcos, and even then Charley had a hard time keeping up with the funny little characters that leapt out of his pen. They were drawn with almost the same economy of line as they are now, thirty years later, and that was a good thing, because they came fast and furious, as prolific and prodigal as Thurber's rabbits and Al Capp's schmoos. On Dr. Grusendorff droned. Genes or conditioning? The weighty professor with the twinkle in his eye dwelt on the knotty question week after week, until one day across the aisle Barsotti slipped me a piece of paper. On it he had drawn a caricature of Dr. Grusendorff debating with himself the great inquiry. Off to one side, dwarfed by the walrus-shaped professor, was a bewhiskered gnome who answered in a small but persistent balloon voice, "Only the grotto knows."

After that, the gnome popped up now and again in Charley's cartoons for the *College Star*, and obviously made a lasting impression on me. I liked it that the word "gnome" had two meanings. One was a fabled fairy, specifically a shriveled old man who lived underground and guarded a treasure. The other was a pithy saying. Of course, "gnome" was my word for the character. Charley simply (or not so simply) drew him and put four words in his mouth. But everything fit. Grotto suggested a cave familiar to the gnome, a cavern that held great truth.

You know how you are at that age. I was convinced Charley Barsotti had a genius, a genie (indeed, dozens!) in him. The shock was trying to talk to him about it. He blinked and feigned (I could not believe he was straight; now I might) puzzlement, said he had no earthly idea what I was about with his cartoons. The only time I felt we had truly confided in one another was when Charley told me he wanted to be a *New Yorker* cartoonist. We were poolside at the Brown School for retarded children, where Charley was a dorm master, and he kept yelling at the kids when they got into the deep end. I too wanted to be at the *New Yorker*, as a writer. I remember, now with rue, thinking that Charley would have a harder time of it than I. He already had a pregnant wife, and to make ends meet they were having to play dormitory Mom and Dad.

But that was something, a Texan even mentioning the *New Yorker* in 1954, much less wanting to draw for it. People forget how backward we were, couldn't have been a hundred subscribers in the whole state. Texas was poor, if you can believe it. Oh, the legend of the land of the big rich rolling in oil and cattle had been stamped upon us for years by the Eastern press, but it was an exaggerated grotesquerie. The fact was there were fewer than ten Texans who had incomes of $1 million or more. Even by 1956, the per capita income in the state was $254 below the national average. From 1929 to 1955 Texas had gone from the thirty-fourth state in personal income to twenty-eighth,only five skips gained in 26 years. Politically, we were about the same speed. A wealthy Southern dandy, Allan Shivers, was governor, and his idol was Senator McCarthy. The year Charley and I were juniors at Southwest Texas State, the guv proposed the death penalty for anyone in Texas convicted of being a member of the Communist party. He was supported so strongly by four of our ten millionaires—H. L. Hunt, Clint Murchison, Sid Richardson, and Hugh Roy Cullen—that the 1954 Gridiron Show of the Women's National Press Club in Washington featured a skit on the Texas vigilante quartet. The chorus sang: "They like to hunt for Commies/And pinks of every hue,/But if they can't find Commies/Plain liberals will do."

The witch hunt even climbed up the ivy and touched our quaint campus in the hills. Dr. Wright, beloved chairman of the English department, a fat man given to flights of poetry, wrote a lightly biting bit of whimsy about the handsome governor receiving some ladies from San Marcos who almost fell over themselves in adoration. The reception had, indeed, taken place. Anyway, Dr. Wright read his naughty poem to his classes. Governor Shivers had him fired. Barsotti wrote me just as this book was going to press: "After Dr. Wright got fired, I tried to do some cartoons about it in the *Star*; my cartoons were carefully screened (hell, censored) by the college president, Dr. Flowers. It was only because the outcast professor's name was Wright that I was able to pun my way through a cartoon of almost mute protest." Satire is the lifeblood of a cartoonist, and Charley Barsotti must have seen the handwriting on the wall. He disappeared, as did Dr. Wright, from our feudal mist and was not seen for years.

Then, lo and behold, he turned up in the *New Yorker* just as he said he would. I don't remember when I first spotted the inimitable Barsotti sketch, but it was middle-age time for us and America. The sixties had just turned into the seventies, and I was in Dallas, an old war-horse newspaperman trying on public television for size. As I read the *New Yorker* and watched Charley's kings, clowns, artists, mutts, deskmen, and barflies do their thing week after week, I created a fantasy about Barsotti. Of course he lived in the Algonquin at 59 West Forty-fourth, dined in a banquette in the Rose Room with colleagues like Brendan Gill and Charles Addams. It was only after lunch that he went to his drawing board in his rooms, which echoed with the ghosts of Mencken, Nathan, Benchley, and Thurber. Then, with a fresh cartoon in hand, Barsotti would make the short walk to the *New Yorker* offices at 28 West Forty-fourth. There he might run into E. B. White, in briefly from his farm, or stop and jaw a bit with Joseph Mitchell, my man. Then it would be back to the venerable Algonquin and its mahogany, brass, and marble and its stiff side-car cocktails. Ah, what a life, what a dream fulfilled.

What a stunner to learn that Charley lived at 419 East Fifty-fifth in KANSAS CITY, MO! For God's sake, he mailed in his cartoons. Only stayed at the Algonquin on the rare occasions he was called to New York to hobnob with editors and the fabled staff. Oh, well.

The curious thing, though, is that once Charley and I got back together (he and Ramoth visit at my farm outside Dallas), I realized that Charley did not live and work in K.C. after all, that the part of him that mattered had been in Manhattan and the Algonquin all the while. And that is as it should be, because it says much about his substance and spirit as a cartoonist. Even as Barsotti breaks out and works in other magazines, such as *Texas Monthly*, his bias toward the American experience is that of the Eastern intellectual as nurtured by primitive genius Harold Ross. No matter that Charley was born and raised in Texas and educated (in a manner of speaking) in San Marcos. The boy and the student, and now the man, were always removed from the rest of us. (He told me recently during a drinking bout that he remembered little from his college years, not his pals, not even his gnome who spoke from the grotto. I was afraid to ask if he remembered me.) No, Charley has never gotten close enough to a chigger to be bitten by one, and he's never had an armadillo by the tail except metaphorically. His sensibilities, if not his manners, are those of the sophisticate, not the native, and the cartoons he does on Texas are those of an outsider (albeit a knowing one) who has come upon a place and a people that readily lend themselves to caricature.

But isn't this the state of any artist anywhere? Faulkner was a stranger in his own hometown even as he lived and died it in life and fiction. He was as much an expatriate of Mississippi as Katherine Anne Porter and Larry McMurtry and Charles Barsotti are of Texas.

Besides,Texas is a caricature, not of itself but its myth, and the myth, until recently, was manufactured in the East, not the West. We are what others make us, and we have been since Texas and the New World first came into European consciousness. The remoteness of the land and its fantastic character continued to thrill and amuse, even as Eastern American journalists began to pick up where the Spanish and French adventurers left off. Everyone who was anyone in Texas came from somewhere else, and they came with extravagant expectations and fulfilled them extravagantly. J. R. Ewing is a Yankee producer's notion of a Texas villain, and the only thing wrong with J. R. is that he is not nearly as mean and as filthy rich as the genuine articles. So when Charley Barsotti comes along with a Hopalong Cassidy grin from Manhattan by way of Kansas City, San Marcos, and Austin, and pokes a little fun at us, he is hardly out of line. The best humor is universal, though necessarily anchored in local color and custom. So what's wrong with a cartoonist taking his favorite funny little king, duding him up in Gucci boots and Ralph Lauren chaps, and setting him loose upon the lonesome prairie as a funny little cowboy? The king came out of the gnome and the gnome came out of . . . Charley? The cowboy is, was, a mythical creature anyway, and Barsotti gives his Texan a droll twist suitable to the modern temper.

The beauty of it is that today we can laugh at ourselves, can even publish from Austin a magazine that does more with the Texas myth than any Eastern outfit ever did. The guy doesn't get offended. Charley doesn't get the ax from *Texas Monthly*, and no one has to slit his own throat in shame. Besides, for those of us who love him, Barsotti is back where he belongs. Well, that may be going too far. Don't panic Charley, but you damn sure don't belong in K.C.

Bill Porterfield

YOU CAN TAKE THE BOY OUT OF TEXAS...

C Barsotti's TEXAS
"... you have free rein so long as it's (about) Texas and it's funny."
FROM A LETTER FROM THE EDITOR.
LET'S SEE, WHAT'S FUNNY ABOUT TEXAS?
HA HA HA HA HA HA HA HA HA
NAW, THAT WON'T DO...
HEE HEE
...EVERYBODY PICKS ON HOUSTON.
© C Barsotti

"Hey, pardner, are you a buckaroo? I'm a buckaroo, and if you want to be a buckaroo I'm the guy to see."

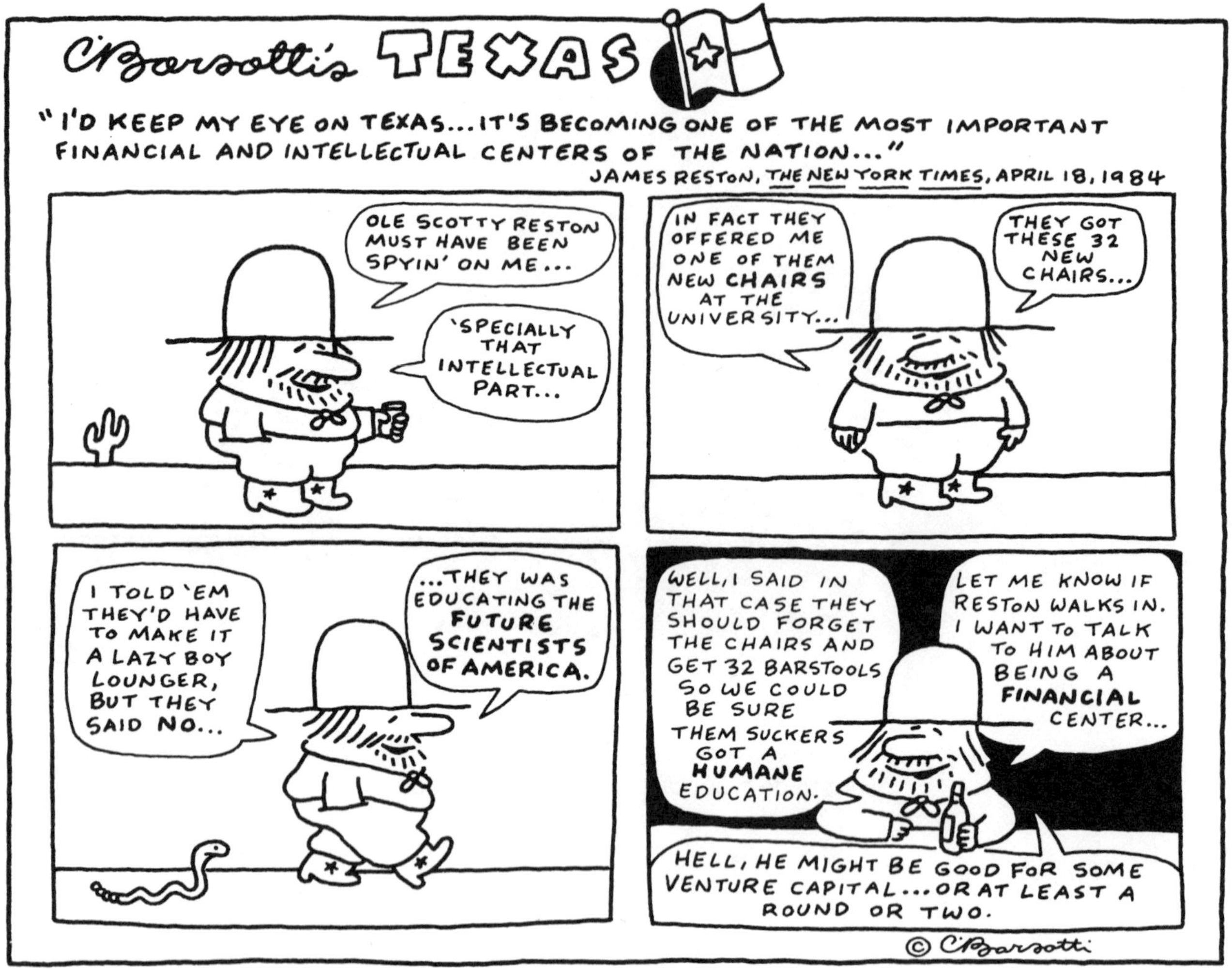
C Barsotti's TEXAS
"I'D KEEP MY EYE ON TEXAS... IT'S BECOMING ONE OF THE MOST IMPORTANT FINANCIAL AND INTELLECTUAL CENTERS OF THE NATION..."
JAMES RESTON, THE NEW YORK TIMES, APRIL 18, 1984
OLE SCOTTY RESTON MUST HAVE BEEN SPYIN' ON ME...
'SPECIALLY THAT INTELLECTUAL PART...
IN FACT THEY OFFERED ME ONE OF THEM NEW CHAIRS AT THE UNIVERSITY...
THEY GOT THESE 32 NEW CHAIRS...
I TOLD 'EM THEY'D HAVE TO MAKE IT A LAZY BOY LOUNGER, BUT THEY SAID NO...
...THEY WAS EDUCATING THE FUTURE SCIENTISTS OF AMERICA.
WELL, I SAID IN THAT CASE THEY SHOULD FORGET THE CHAIRS AND GET 32 BARSTOOLS SO WE COULD BE SURE THEM SUCKERS GOT A HUMANE EDUCATION.
LET ME KNOW IF RESTON WALKS IN. I WANT TO TALK TO HIM ABOUT BEING A FINANCIAL CENTER...
HELL, HE MIGHT BE GOOD FOR SOME VENTURE CAPITAL... OR AT LEAST A ROUND OR TWO.
© C Barsotti

TEACH YOU
HOW TO
HOO-RAW.
$1
C. Barsotti

COWBOY PSYCHIATRIST
THAT'S RIGHT, DON'T DENY YOURSELF YOUR FEELINGS.
C Barsotti

"Well, at least you're out and about. When I'm depressed I just roll up into a ball."

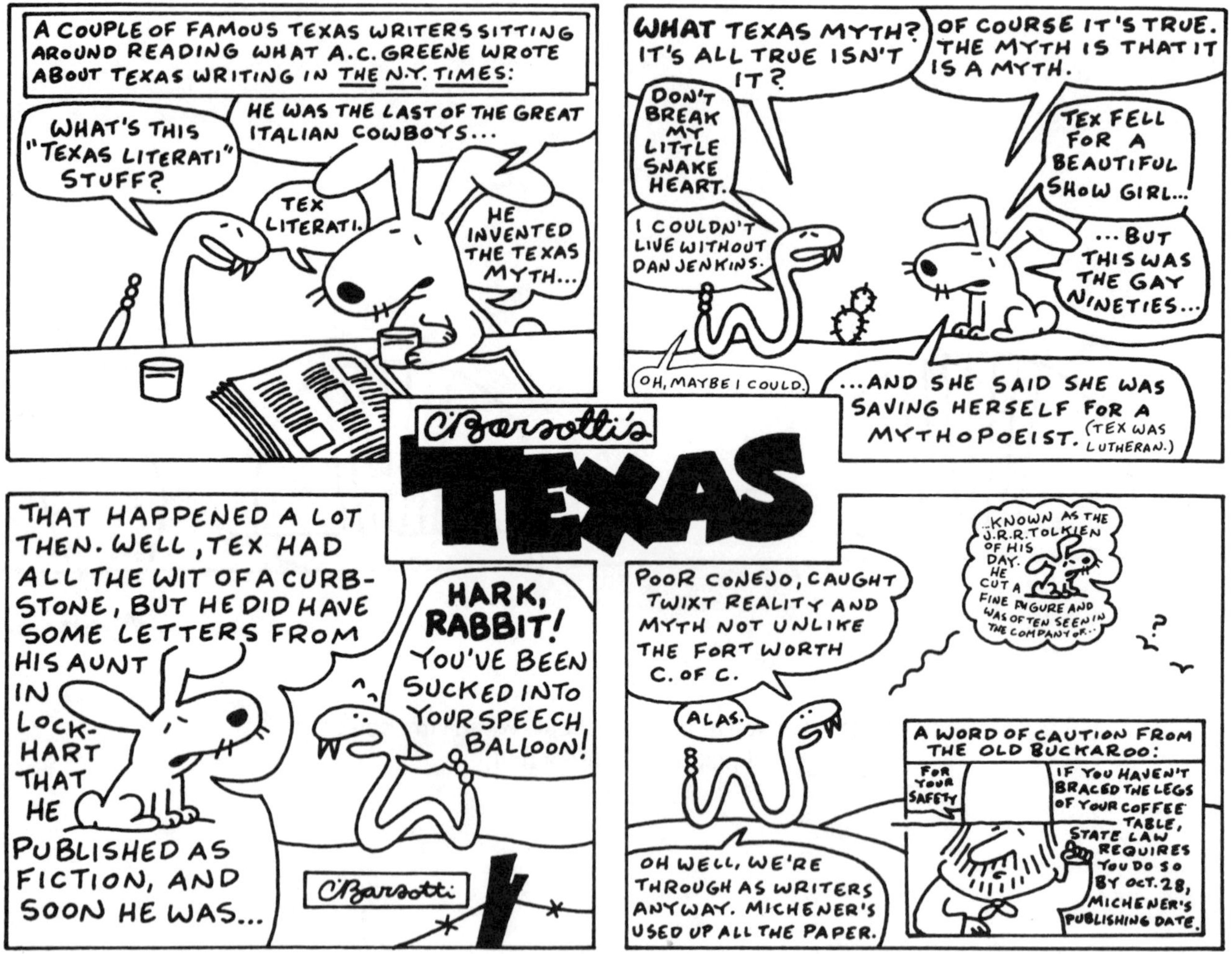

A COUPLE OF FAMOUS TEXAS WRITERS SITTING AROUND READING WHAT A.C. GREENE WROTE ABOUT TEXAS WRITING IN THE N.Y. TIMES:
WHAT'S THIS "TEXAS LITERATI" STUFF?
HE WAS THE LAST OF THE GREAT ITALIAN COWBOYS...
TEX LITERATI.
HE INVENTED THE TEXAS MYTH...
WHAT TEXAS MYTH? IT'S ALL TRUE ISN'T IT?
OF COURSE IT'S TRUE. THE MYTH IS THAT IT IS A MYTH.
DON'T BREAK MY LITTLE SNAKE HEART.
TEX FELL FOR A BEAUTIFUL SHOW GIRL...
I COULDN'T LIVE WITHOUT DAN JENKINS.
...BUT THIS WAS THE GAY NINETIES...
OH, MAYBE I COULD.
...AND SHE SAID SHE WAS SAVING HERSELF FOR A MYTHOPOEIST. (TEX WAS LUTHERAN.)
C. Barsotti's TEXAS
THAT HAPPENED A LOT THEN. WELL, TEX HAD ALL THE WIT OF A CURB-STONE, BUT HE DID HAVE SOME LETTERS FROM HIS AUNT IN LOCK-HART THAT HE PUBLISHED AS FICTION, AND SOON HE WAS...
HARK, RABBIT! YOU'VE BEEN SUCKED INTO YOUR SPEECH BALLOON!
C. Barsotti
...KNOWN AS THE J.R.R. TOLKIEN OF HIS DAY. HE CUT A FINE FIGURE AND WAS OFTEN SEEN IN THE COMPANY OF...
POOR CONEJO, CAUGHT TWIXT REALITY AND MYTH NOT UNLIKE THE FORT WORTH C. OF C.
ALAS.
?
OH WELL, WE'RE THROUGH AS WRITERS ANYWAY. MICHENER'S USED UP ALL THE PAPER.
A WORD OF CAUTION FROM THE OLD BUCKAROO:
FOR YOUR SAFETY
IF YOU HAVEN'T BRACED THE LEGS OF YOUR COFFEE TABLE, STATE LAW REQUIRES YOU DO SO BY OCT. 28, MICHENER'S PUBLISHING DATE.

THE SUN-BELT KID
I CAN'T WALK ANOTHER STEP...
...THESE DAMN BOOTS ARE KILLING ME.
CBarsotti

MAKE BIG MONEY IN WESTERN ART.
C. Barsotti

PERHAPS SOME COWBOY BOOTS.
CBarsotti

URBAN SINGING COWBOY
LOST MY HEART IN A GRIDLOCK
CBarsotti

"I just want you to know, Elwood, if I'd been looking for a good guy tonight I'd have gone to a Roy Rogers movie."

THE CODE OF THE WEST

* LET'S SEE MICHENER COME UP WITH SOME FANCY LETTERING LIKE THAT.

THE EXISTENTIALIST

RAMBLIN' MAN

THE OLD COWBOY MOVED FROM PLACE TO PLACE AND WAS NEVER TOO LONG IN ONE PLACE. SAN ANTONIO, FORT WORTH, EL PASO, AND PLACES FORGOTTEN AND PLACES WITHOUT NAMES HAD ALL BEEN HOME.
NOW IT WAS SATURDAY NIGHT.
PHOOEY.
CBarsotti

THE SAD STORY OF THE LAD FROM LULING WHO WENT WRONG

THE LONE PRAIRIE

"Could you direct me to a vest
pocket park, please?"

“Here’s a little song I wrote when I heard the Village Voice was bought by a birdseed salesman.”

"It was three years ago today that Clovis went out West for the big chili cook-off and was never heard from again."

WORK-IN-PROGRESS

COWBOY ACCOUNTANT
WELL, HELL, SOMEBODY'S GOT TO KEEP THE DAMN BOOKS.
CBarsotti

THE TRUTH ABOUT THE SUN BELT

COWBOY WHO NEVER LEARNED TO HUNKER DOWN

OUTLAW
I PROBABLY OUGHT TO GO OUT AND PUT ANOTHER DIME IN THE METER.
AW, THE HELL WITH IT.
CBarsotti

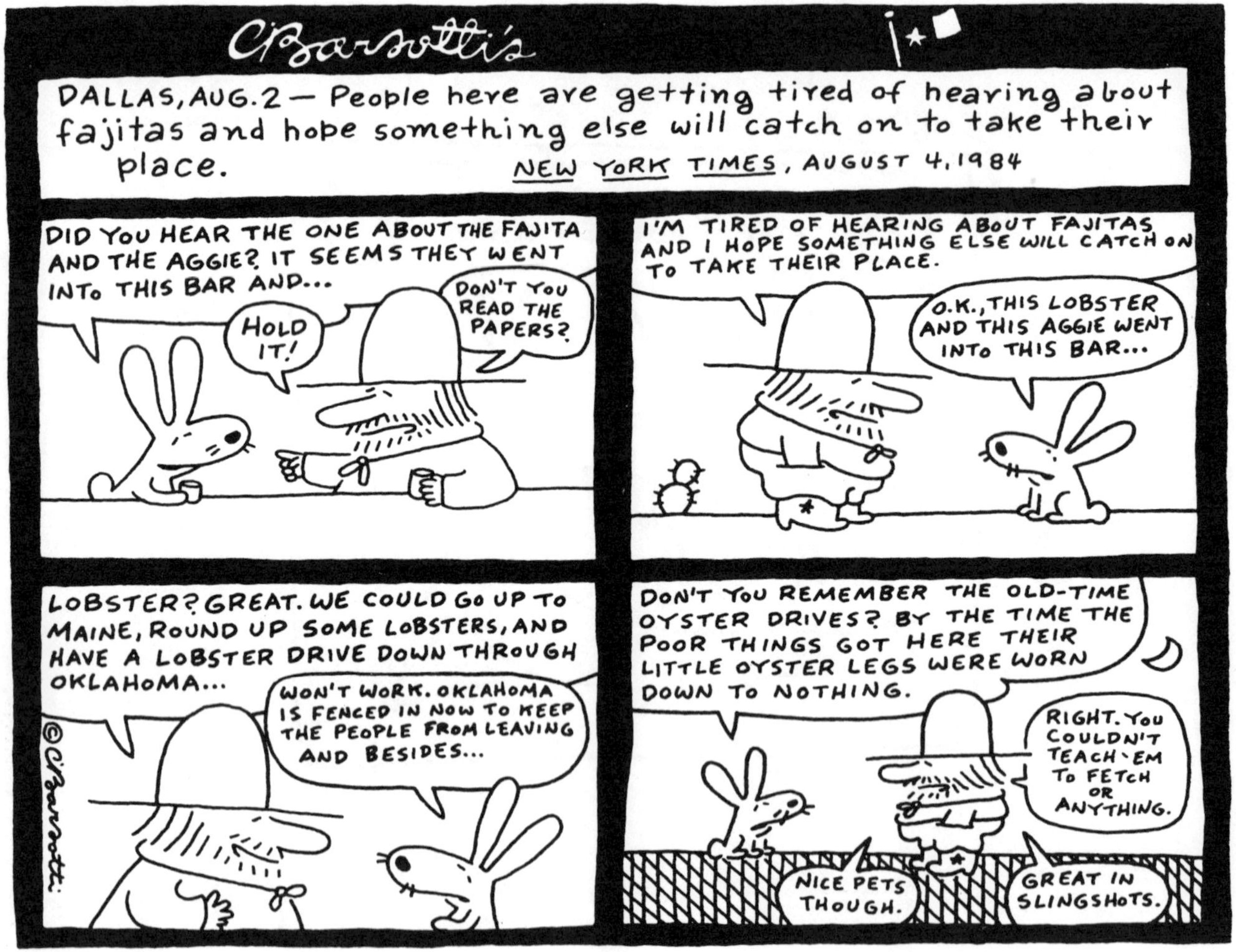
C. Barsotti's
DALLAS, AUG. 2 — People here are getting tired of hearing about fajitas and hope something else will catch on to take their place. NEW YORK TIMES, AUGUST 4, 1984
DID YOU HEAR THE ONE ABOUT THE FAJITA AND THE AGGIE? IT SEEMS THEY WENT INTO THIS BAR AND...
HOLD IT!
DON'T YOU READ THE PAPERS?
I'M TIRED OF HEARING ABOUT FAJITAS AND I HOPE SOMETHING ELSE WILL CATCH ON TO TAKE THEIR PLACE.
O.K., THIS LOBSTER AND THIS AGGIE WENT INTO THIS BAR...
LOBSTER? GREAT. WE COULD GO UP TO MAINE, ROUND UP SOME LOBSTERS, AND HAVE A LOBSTER DRIVE DOWN THROUGH OKLAHOMA...
WON'T WORK. OKLAHOMA IS FENCED IN NOW TO KEEP THE PEOPLE FROM LEAVING AND BESIDES...
© C. Barsotti
DON'T YOU REMEMBER THE OLD-TIME OYSTER DRIVES? BY THE TIME THE POOR THINGS GOT HERE THEIR LITTLE OYSTER LEGS WERE WORN DOWN TO NOTHING.
RIGHT. YOU COULDN'T TEACH 'EM TO FETCH OR ANYTHING.
NICE PETS THOUGH.
GREAT IN SLINGSHOTS.

COOKING WITH MESQUITE

PRIVATE LIVES OF THE LEGENDS OF TEXAS

FERN BAR

HELL, MIGHT AS WELL HAVE A BEER WITH THE GUERILLAS IN EL SALVADOR.
CBarsotti

OUR ORAL HISTORY– WILL IT BE LOST?

CBarsotti

"Now I'd like to sing you a little song I wrote while drunk as a skunk."

"Gene 'n' Hoppy 'n' Roy rode through once, but they was just looking for a Dairy Queen."

LAW OF THE WEST

BAD GUYS OF THE OLD WEST

SAGEBRUSH REBELLION

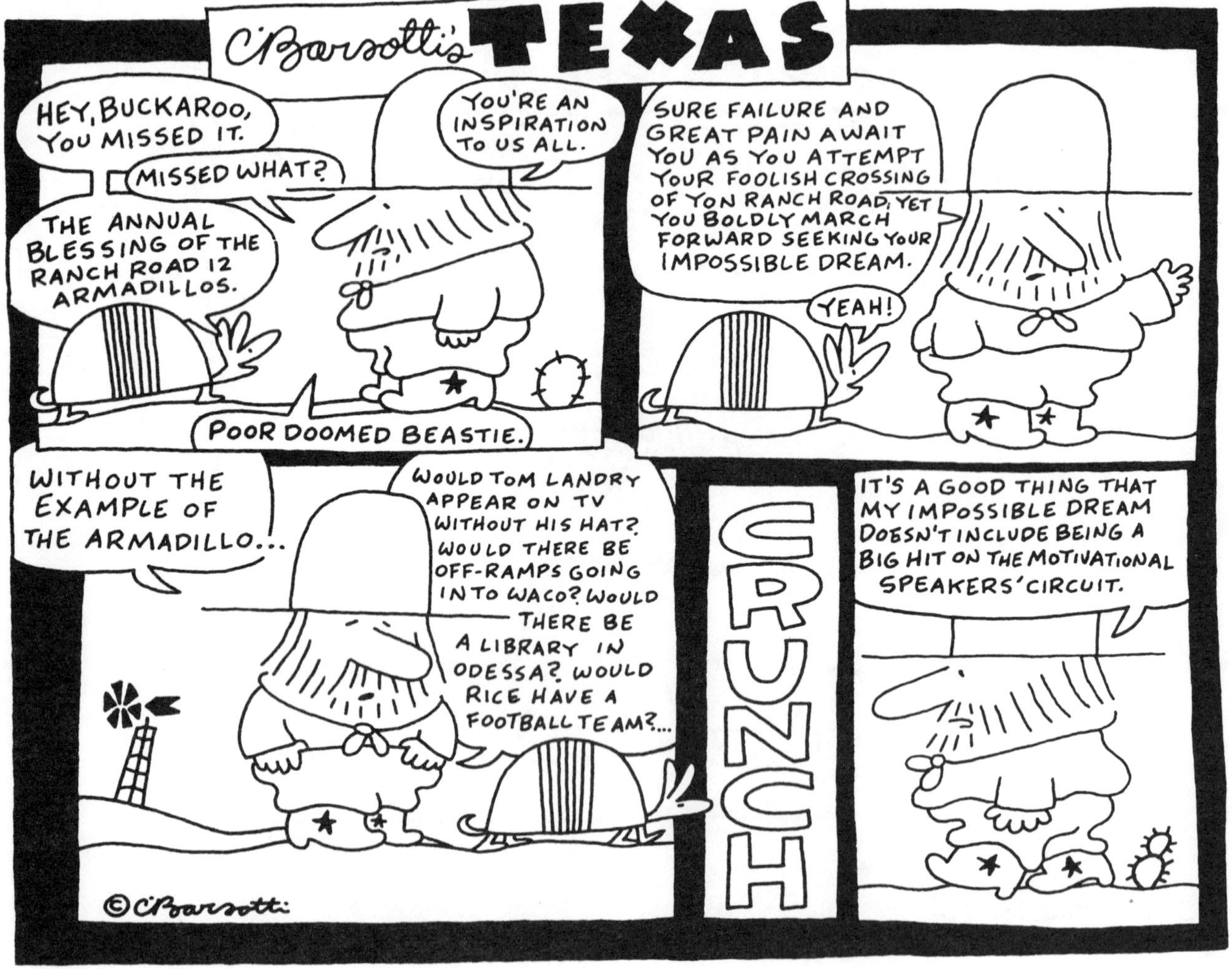
C. Barsotti's TEXAS
HEY, BUCKAROO, YOU MISSED IT.
MISSED WHAT?
THE ANNUAL BLESSING OF THE RANCH ROAD 12 ARMADILLOS.
YOU'RE AN INSPIRATION TO US ALL.
POOR DOOMED BEASTIE.
SURE FAILURE AND GREAT PAIN AWAIT YOU AS YOU ATTEMPT YOUR FOOLISH CROSSING OF YON RANCH ROAD; YET YOU BOLDLY MARCH FORWARD SEEKING YOUR IMPOSSIBLE DREAM.
YEAH!
WITHOUT THE EXAMPLE OF THE ARMADILLO...
WOULD TOM LANDRY APPEAR ON TV WITHOUT HIS HAT? WOULD THERE BE OFF-RAMPS GOING INTO WACO? WOULD THERE BE A LIBRARY IN ODESSA? WOULD RICE HAVE A FOOTBALL TEAM?...
©C. Barsotti
CRUNCH
IT'S A GOOD THING THAT MY IMPOSSIBLE DREAM DOESN'T INCLUDE BEING A BIG HIT ON THE MOTIVATIONAL SPEAKERS' CIRCUIT.

CHILI WEATHER

"Here's a song I wrote about fifteen minutes ago when my little gal left me for a bi-sexual backstage caterer."

WILD BILL'S ANXIETY ATTACK

C. Barsotti's
TEXAS
HEY, CONEJO, ARE YOU ALL READY FOR THE SESQUICENTENNIAL?
I'M UP TO THE SECOND SYLLABLE.
"CESS-KWI." WHAT COMES NEXT?
SIN.
BUT ONLY IF YOU GET INVITED TO THE RIGHT PARTIES.
THAT SILLY ARMADILLO GETS INVITED EVERYWHERE.
SOME OFFICIAL MASCOT. HE'S NEVER COME OUT OF HIS SHELL.
TEXAS
CESS-KWI-SIN-TIN-E-EL
BUT I WOULD HAVE BEEN GREAT.
THE OL' BUCKAROO SEZ:
REMEMBER, TRUE RANGERS ATTEND ONLY OFFICIALLY SANCTIONED SESQUI-CENTENNIAL EVENTS.
IF WE ALL WORK TOGETHER, WE CAN KEEP THE SIN OUT OF THE SESQUI-TENNIAL.
RABBIT, YOU COULD GIVE BOOSTERISM A BAD NAME.
BUT YOUR OFFICIALLY SANCTIONED BOOTS ARE REALLY SPIFFY.
I'VE LEARNED MY LESSON.
NOTE: THIS IS NOT THE OFFICIALLY SANCTIONED MASCOT OF THE TEXAS 1986 SEZQUINTESSENTIAL. IT WILL BE SEEN BY TRUE RANGERS AS AN EXAMPLE OF ANARCHISTIC MOCKERY.

"Oh, I don't mind being referred to as prehistoric, the important thing is I don't feel prehistoric."

HOME IS THE WANDERER
NOW THAT'S CHILI.
CBarsotti

TEXAS CHIC

SOON AS I FINISH THIS I BELIEVE I'LL GO BUY A PAIR OF TOP-SIDERS.
CBarsotti

SAGEBRUSH REBELLION
I'M NOT RIDING ANY DAMN MECHANICAL BULL.
CBarsotti.

"Where is it written that we accountants
can't express our individuality?"

"Hey, pal, do you want to hear how the West was won?"

GREAT IDEAS OF WESTERN MAN

"Now here's a number that I know all you outlaws
out there are going to relate to real good."

RENEGADE

MY DINNER WITH BILLY BOB
HERE, HAVE A FRITO.
CBarsotti

SECRET
OF
MY
CHILI
$1
CBarsotti

HAT PINS
FINLANDIA VODKA
EAST HAMPTON
HÄAGEN:DAZS ICE CREAM
NEW SCHOOL
CBarsotti

SUNSTROKE

"No, first you agree that we can agree to disagree,
then we'll talk politics."

TIME AN ENDLESS SONG

C Barsotti's TEXAS
ARTICLE HERE IN THE NEW YORK TIMES ABOUT AUSTIN. A FELLA'S QUOTED SAYING, "THERE IS REAL PRESSURE ON THE URBAN ANIMALS..."
OF COURSE, WHY ELSE WAS THE MARTINI INVENTED?
I THINK THE FELLA WAS TALKING ABOUT VARMINTS, REAL ANIMALS.
WELL, AS LONG AS HE DIDN'T MENTION ANY EDITORS BY NAME, I GUESS IT'S OK.
ACTUALLY, THE PRESSURE'S BEEN GETTING TO ME.
I'M A WRECK.
BUT YOU'RE A CELEBRITY. EVERY WEEK ON "AUSTIN CITY LIMITS" THEY SING ABOUT GOIN' HOME TO TH' ARMADILLO.
YEAH, ON PBS. HOW'D YOU LIKE ALL THESE MASTERPIECE THEATER TYPES DROPPING BY TO VISIT YOU ALL THE TIME? I KEEP RUNNING OUT OF WINE AND BRIE.
AND IF I NEVER SEE A VOLVO STATION WAGON AGAIN IT'LL BE TOO SOON.
REALLY SWELL. EVERYBODY WANTS TO GO HOME TO THE ARMADILLO, BUT DOES ANYBODY EVER INVITE THE POOR OL' ARMADILLO HOME? I ASK YOU, HAS MARK WHITE EVER SAID, COME OVER FOR DINNER, WE'LL GO OUT IN THE LAWN AND DIG UP SOME ROOTS?
WELL, HANG IN THERE. WITH THE BUDGET THE WAY IT IS, HE MIGHT.
© C Barsotti

THE MISFIT

TOO DAMN BAD LARRY HART NEVER WROTE ANY LYRICS FOR COUNTRY MUSIC.
CBarsotti

"I had to change the name of this next song when
the lady's husband threatened to kill me."

"I'm a good guy, ma'm, as you can tell by my pleasant countenance."

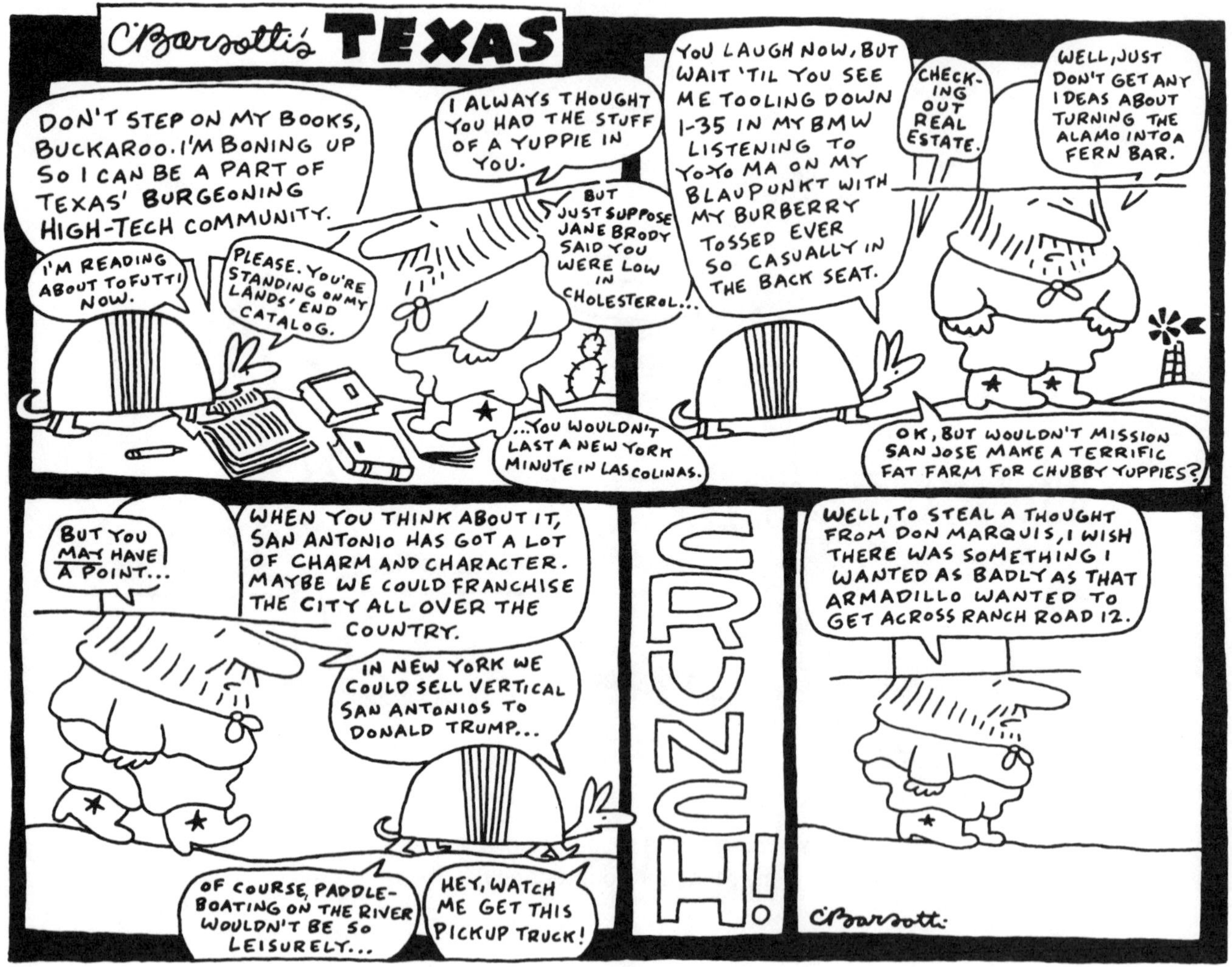
C. Barsotti's TEXAS
DON'T STEP ON MY BOOKS, BUCKAROO. I'M BONING UP SO I CAN BE A PART OF TEXAS' BURGEONING HIGH-TECH COMMUNITY.
I ALWAYS THOUGHT YOU HAD THE STUFF OF A YUPPIE IN YOU.
BUT JUST SUPPOSE JANE BRODY SAID YOU WERE LOW IN CHOLESTEROL...
I'M READING ABOUT TOFUTTI NOW.
PLEASE. YOU'RE STANDING ON MY LANDS' END CATALOG.
...YOU WOULDN'T LAST A NEW YORK MINUTE IN LAS COLINAS.
YOU LAUGH NOW, BUT WAIT 'TIL YOU SEE ME TOOLING DOWN I-35 IN MY BMW LISTENING TO YO-YO MA ON MY BLAUPUNKT WITH MY BURBERRY TOSSED EVER SO CASUALLY IN THE BACK SEAT.
CHECKING OUT REAL ESTATE.
WELL, JUST DON'T GET ANY IDEAS ABOUT TURNING THE ALAMO INTO A FERN BAR.
OK, BUT WOULDN'T MISSION SAN JOSE MAKE A TERRIFIC FAT FARM FOR CHUBBY YUPPIES?
BUT YOU MAY HAVE A POINT...
WHEN YOU THINK ABOUT IT, SAN ANTONIO HAS GOT A LOT OF CHARM AND CHARACTER. MAYBE WE COULD FRANCHISE THE CITY ALL OVER THE COUNTRY.
IN NEW YORK WE COULD SELL VERTICAL SAN ANTONIOS TO DONALD TRUMP...
OF COURSE, PADDLE-BOATING ON THE RIVER WOULDN'T BE SO LEISURELY...
HEY, WATCH ME GET THIS PICKUP TRUCK!
CRUNCH!
WELL, TO STEAL A THOUGHT FROM DON MARQUIS, I WISH THERE WAS SOMETHING I WANTED AS BADLY AS THAT ARMADILLO WANTED TO GET ACROSS RANCH ROAD 12.
C. Barsotti

EASTWARD HO!

HAPPY TRAILS
THAT SIBELIUS, WHAT AN HOMBRE.

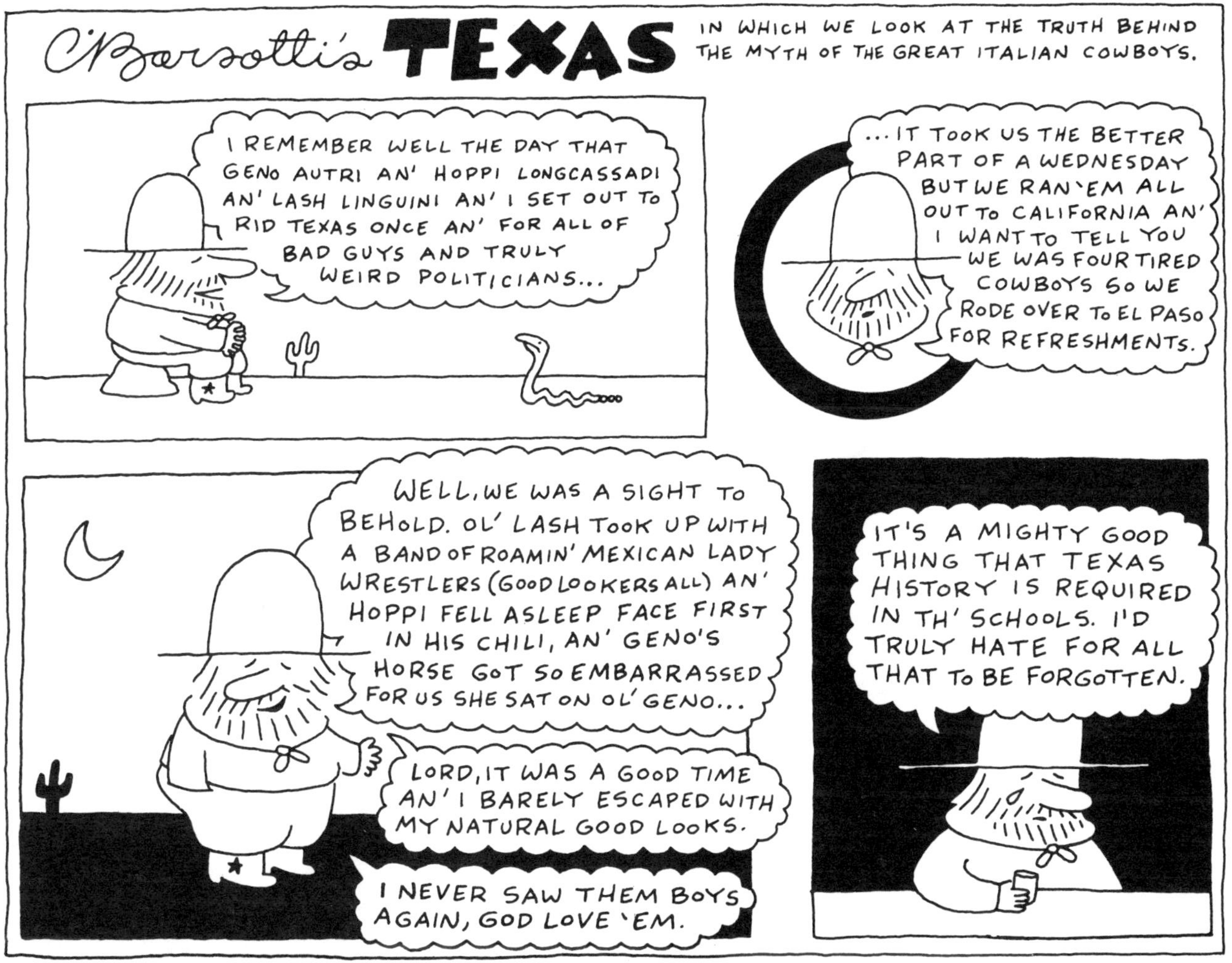

Barsotti's TEXAS
IN WHICH WE LOOK AT THE TRUTH BEHIND THE MYTH OF THE GREAT ITALIAN COWBOYS.
I REMEMBER WELL THE DAY THAT GENO AUTRI AN' HOPPI LONGCASSADI AN' LASH LINGUINI AN' I SET OUT TO RID TEXAS ONCE AN' FOR ALL OF BAD GUYS AND TRULY WEIRD POLITICIANS...
...IT TOOK US THE BETTER PART OF A WEDNESDAY BUT WE RAN'EM ALL OUT TO CALIFORNIA AN' I WANT TO TELL YOU WE WAS FOUR TIRED COWBOYS SO WE RODE OVER TO EL PASO FOR REFRESHMENTS.
WELL, WE WAS A SIGHT TO BEHOLD. OL' LASH TOOK UP WITH A BAND OF ROAMIN' MEXICAN LADY WRESTLERS (GOOD LOOKERS ALL) AN' HOPPI FELL ASLEEP FACE FIRST IN HIS CHILI, AN' GENO'S HORSE GOT SO EMBARRASSED FOR US SHE SAT ON OL' GENO...
LORD, IT WAS A GOOD TIME AN' I BARELY ESCAPED WITH MY NATURAL GOOD LOOKS.
I NEVER SAW THEM BOYS AGAIN, GOD LOVE 'EM.
IT'S A MIGHTY GOOD THING THAT TEXAS HISTORY IS REQUIRED IN TH' SCHOOLS. I'D TRULY HATE FOR ALL THAT TO BE FORGOTTEN.

COWBOY NEWS

EARLIER TODAY GENE ROUNDED UP SIX DESPERADOES JUST OUTSIDE ABILENE. HOPPY SAVED A RUNAWAY STAGE COACH, AND ROY AND THE BOYS...
CBarsotti

"You've been selected to appear in the forthcoming edition of 'Who's Who on the Lone Prairie.'"

C. Barsotti's TEXAS
HEY, BUCKAROO, YOU WANT TO PLAY A GAME OF **TEXAS TRIVIA?**
TEXAS **TRIVIA?** THERE'S NO SUCH THING.
OKLAHOMA FOR SURE.
WHOLE DAMN STATE IS TRIVIAL.
I'VE GOT A TRIVIA QUESTION FOR YOU THOUGH. WHAT GREAT COMPOSER WAS BORN IN WACO?
GIVE UP?
FRANZ JOSEPH HAYDN.
YOU DIDN'T KNOW **THAT?**
USED TO BE A BIG SIGN OUT ON THE HIGHWAY THAT SAID, "**THE BIRTHPLACE OF FRANZ JOSEPH HAYDN, NO KIDDING**."
YOU **KNOW** THEY NEVER KID IN WACO.
IT'S NOT ZONED FOR JOSHING.
THEY GOT TO SLIP OVER TO AUSTIN.
LOTS OF JOSHING IN AUSTIN.
© C. Barsotti
I PROBABLY OUGHT TO PLAY THAT GUY SOME TRIVIA.
I KNOW LOTS OF STUFF.
I'LL BET **HE** DOESN'T KNOW WHAT YEAR ROSSINI WROTE "SAN ANTONIO ROSE".

HOME ON THE RANGE

UNCLE ED WENT OUT WEST AND BECAME A COWBOY.

"Now the boys and I would like to sing you a little number."

LONESOME COWBOY
WHERE THE HELL IS EVERYONE?
CBarsotti

GREAT IDEAS OF WESTERN MAN

ALL HAT AND NO CATTLE

COWBOY IN ENGLAND

WESTERN ART CRITIC
CBarsotti

THE OLD COWBOY SEEKS HIS FORTUNE.

"Louis, the bluebonnets are rampant on the hillsides; should we in the spirit of Spring be doing less?"

CATFISH

A MAN'S GOT TO DO WHAT A MAN'S GOT TO DO.

1

CROSSOVER

HERE'S A LITTLE NUMBER ABOUT THE DE STIJL EXHIBITION AT THE WALKER ART CENTER IN MINNEAPOLIS.
CBarsotti

WESTERN ART

IT'LL BE A RELIEF TO GO BACK TO PUNCHING COWS AFTER THIS.
C.Barsotti

C Barsotti's
TEXAS
"That sort of intangible drive, like the one behind northern California's revolutionary silicon chip, might make Austin the nation's 'brain cell'..." FROM USA TODAY
INTANGIBLE DRIVE?
IT'S JUST OFF BEN WHITE BLVD. IT'S WHERE THEY KEEP THE NATION'S BRAIN CELL.
IN A SLURPEE CUP AT A 7-ELEVEN.
TOURISTS COME FROM ALL OVER.
POLITICIANS TRIED TO COME FOR PHOTO-OPPORTUNITIES, BUT THE BRAIN CELL HID IN A TWINKIE.
WOW! DO THEY SHOW IT ON "AUSTIN CITY LIMITS"?
IN THE OPENING CLIPS, BUT IT GOES BY PRETTY FAST. ONCE JERRY JEFF WALKER NEARLY STEPPED ON IT. NOW THEY DON'T LET SINGERS ANYWHERE NEAR IT.
EDITORS EITHER. IT LOVES CARTOONISTS THOUGH.
HOW COME IT'S NOT IN DALLAS OR HOUSTON?
WELL, IT IS A BRAIN CELL.
HOWEVER, IT DID ESCAPE TO SAN ANTONIO ONCE. THEY FOUND IT ON THE RIVERWALK WITH A COUPLE OF S.W.T. CHEERLEADERS AND A KNAPSACK FULL OF BARBECUE FROM LOCKHART.
© C Barsotti
HOLD IT!
I'M A TEXAS HUMOR RANGER! THIS MUST STOP!
THEY ONLY SENT ONE RANGER?
WE SHOULD BE PROUD TO HAVE A BRAIN CELL IN AUSTIN.
PHOOEY, I'M GOING OUT TO RANCH ROAD 12...
IT USUALLY TAKES 5 OR 6 PER CARTOONIST.
...AND RUN OVER A PICKUP TRUCK.

"Now I ain't no spangled, rhinestone cowboy,
I'm the real thing."

GRACEFULLY EXITING A BAR IN ODESSA

SAGEBRUSH REBELLION

TEXAS MYTH

I'LL KNOCK THIS SUCKER BACK, HOP IN MY PICKUP, AND GO SEE THE GENE AUTRY FILM FESTIVAL.
C Barsotti

RUGGED INDIVIDUALIST

"Why, looky here. H-33, that's me and the boys."

SAN ANTONIO ROSE

TEXAS
NO MORE LOLLYGAGGING AROUND! TODAY'S THE DAY!
YES, THIS IS THE DAY OUR HERO, MAYNARD, THE YOUNG URBAN EXECUTIVE TRAINEE, BEGINS HIS QUEST!
HOUSTON CITY LIMITS
YESSIR, TODAY I FIND MY TRUE LOVE...
WELCOME TO AUSTIN
TODAY SOMEWHERE, SOMEHOW, WHOEVER SHE IS, I'M GONNA FIND MY LOVE...
...THE TEXAS CHAINSAW CHEERLEADER!
WACO 5 MILES
BOYOHBOY! WE'RE GONNA BE SO HAPPY! WE'RE GONNA BE SO SILLY! WE'RE GONNA LAUGH AND GIGGLE ALL THE TIME! I CAN'T WAIT 'TIL I FIND HER!
DALLAS CITY LIMITS
OH, THE POOR THING!
IT'S TOO LATE.
SHE'S BEEN CAPTURED BY YANKEES!
WELCOME TO CHICAGO
MORAL:
LIKE ASPHALT, YOU CAN COVER A LOT OF GROUND AND STILL BE AS DUMB AS WHEN YOU STARTED.

"Now this nickname, Wild Bill, where in
the hell did you get that?"

SAD MUSIC
CBarsotti

"Here's a little song I wrote when my first love took his leave and the South Presa bus dragged me six blocks."

THE FRIENDLY WEST
HOT ENOUGH FOR YOU, BILL?
HOTTER'N AUNT NELL AT A TENT MEETING.
CBarsotti

C. Barsotti's CAREFULLY RESEARCHED TEXAS
"THIS KIND OF CACTUS DOES NOT GROW IN TEXAS."
MESSAGE FROM THE FACT-CHECKING DEPT. OF TEXAS MONTHLY
SO...
THE CARTOONIST
...WHO SAID IT DID?
BESIDES, WE MUST LEARN TO LOOK BEYOND MERE FACTS TO LARGER TRUTHS.
SMART FELLOW.
VERY WISE.
GOOD-LOOKING TOO.
NEXT TIME I'M IN AUSTIN I GOTTA HAVE A BEER WITH THOSE FACT-CHECKING FOLKS.
STRAIGHTEN 'EM OUT, SOFTEN 'EM UP.
EITHER THAT OR LEARN HOW TO DRAW PRICKLY PEAR.
WHAT DOES IT ALL MEAN?
A RATTLED SNAKE
I KNEW A PRICKLY PAIR ONCE. IT'S THE KIDS THAT SUFFER.
© C. Barsotti